PREDATOR VS PREY

Shark Vs Penguin

Mary Meinking

www.raintreepublishers.co.uk
Visit our website to find out
more information about
Raintree books.

To order:
☎ Phone 0845 6044371
🗎 Fax +44 (0) 1865 312263
💻 Email myorders@raintreepublishers.co.uk

Customers from outside the UK please telephone +44 1865 312262

Raintree is an imprint of Capstone Global Library Limited,
a company incorporated in England and Wales having its
registered office at 7 Pilgrim Street, London, EC4V 6LB
– Registered company number: 6695582

Edited by Rebecca Rissman, Dan Nunn,
    and Catherine Veitch
Designed by Joanna Hinton Malivoire
Levelling by Jeanne Clidas
Picture research by Hannah Taylor
Production by Victoria Fitzgerald
Originated by Capstone Global Library
Printed and bound in China by CTPS

ISBN 978 1 406 21867 1
14 13 12 11 10
10 9 8 7 6 5 4 3 2 1

British Library Cataloguing in Publication Data
Meinking, Mary.
Shark vs penguin. -- (Predator vs prey)
591.5'3-dc22
A full catalogue record for this book is available from the
British Library.

Acknowledgements
We would like to thank the following for permission
to reproduce photographs: Alamy Images pp. 10
(©AfriPics.com), 24 (©AfriPics.com), 25 (©AfriPics.com),
29 (© Visual&Written SL); ardea.com p. 8 (Valerie Taylor);
Corbis pp. 11 (Kevin Schafer), 20 (Tom Brakefield),
21 (Ralph A. Clevenger), 28 (Keren Su); FLPA pp. 9
(Minden Pictures/ Mike Parry), 12 (Minden Pictures/
Fred Bavendam), 15 (Minden Pictures/ Stephen Belcher),
19 (Minden Pictures/ Stephen Belcher); Getty Images
pp. 16 (Gerald Hinde), 22 (National Geographic/ Joel
Sartore); istockphoto pp. 5 (© Dr Awie Badenhorst), 6 (©
Leicafoto), 7 (© Werner Janse van Rensburg); naturepl.
com pp. 26 (Tom Walmsley); Photolibrary pp. 4 (Oxford
Scientific/ David B Fleetham), 14 (Martin Harvey), 17
(Animals Animals/James Watt), 18 (imagebroker.net/ Ingo
Schulz), 23 (WaterFrame/ Reinhard Dirscherl), 27 (Kelvin
Aitken); Reuters p. 13 (Ho New).

Cover photographs of a great white shark reproduced
with permission of FLPA (Minden Pictures/ Mike Parry),
and a South African penguin reproduced with permission
of Alamy (© Nigel Hicks).

We would like to thank Michael Bright for his invaluable
help in the preparation of this book.

Every effort has been made to contact copyright holders
of material reproduced in this book. Any omissions will
be rectified in subsequent printings if notice is given to
the publisher.

Some words are shown in bold, **like this**. You can find
out what they mean by looking in the glossary.

Contents

Going teeth to beak

Jaws snap! Flippers splash! Two animals battle in the deep blue sea. Here's the world's most dangerous fish, the great white shark. It's up against a waddling challenger, the penguin.

shark

penguin

5

These animals live along Africa's coastline. Both have strengths that will help them in this battle.

PREDATOR
great white shark

LENGTH: 460 centimetres

WEIGHT: 1800 kilograms

COVERED IN: rough skin

Key

where great white sharks and African penguins live

PREY
African penguin

LENGTH: 61 centimetres

WEIGHT: 3 kilograms

COVERED IN: short, stiff feathers

Africa

Hunting machine

The shark zooms through the water after its **prey**. It is pointed on both ends like an aeroplane. It steers with its two wing-like **pectoral** fins.

pectoral fin

DID YOU KNOW?

Great whites have rows of saw-like teeth. When a tooth falls out a new one moves into its place. They will have 3,000 teeth during their life.

Water wings

The penguin is a bird but it can't fly. Instead it soars through the water. The penguin's wings are paddle-like flippers.

DID YOU KNOW?

African penguins are also called jackass penguins because they sound like donkeys. Hee-haw!

Who's hungry?

The shark is a **carnivore**, or an animal that eats other animals. Sometimes the shark bumps into **prey** before it eats it. Special **cells** on its snout tell how things will taste by how they feel.

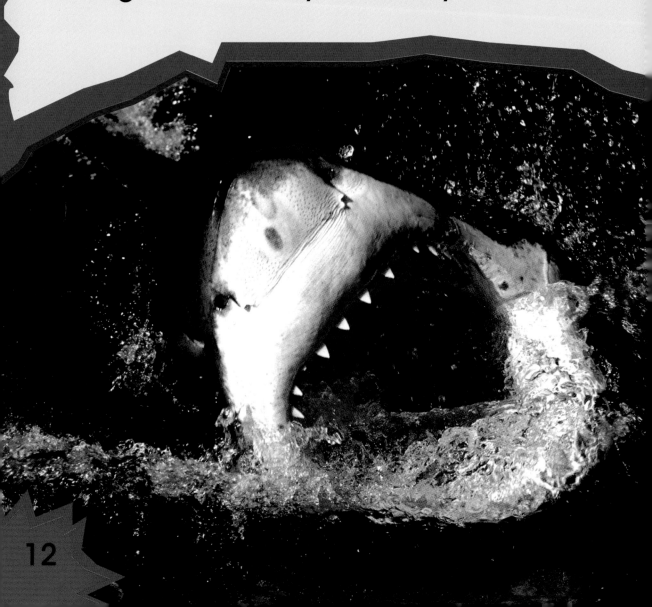

DID YOU KNOW?

Sharks eat almost anything! Great whites eat fish, seals, turtles, and even whales. Some have even eaten cans, car number plates, and surfboards.

surfboard

Sneak attack

The penguin slides into the sea. It swims with its group and hunts for fish. The shark feels the **vibration**, or movement, of the penguins in the water. The shark moves towards them.

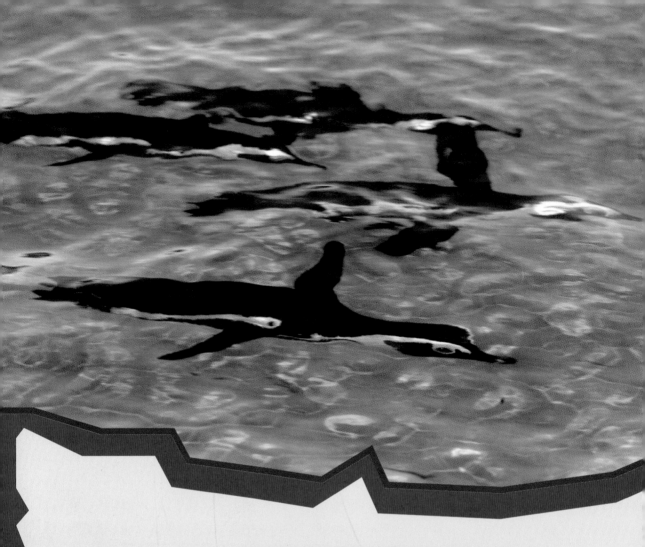

The penguin is **camouflaged**. Fish swimming under the penguin can't see its white belly that **blends** into the sky. Fish above the penguin can't see its black back that blends in with the dark sea bottom.

The shark smells or tastes the water as it searches for food.

The shark swims under the penguins, looking for one that is alone. The shark finds one! Its powerful tail pushes it through the water. The shark's eyes roll back just as it slams into the penguin. They both shoot into the air!

They come splashing down. The startled penguin swims away from the shark. Its flippers flap two times every second to shoot through the water. But the giant shark is on its tail!

DID YOU KNOW?

African penguins can swim at 24 kilometres per hour. That's three times faster than Olympic champions swim. But great whites can swim at 56 kilometres per hour!

The penguin uses its tail and feet to turn quickly. It **zigzags**, or swims in a Z-shaped pattern. It's trying to lose the shark. The shark stays with the penguin. It uses its **pectoral** fins to turn. But the shark can't turn as sharply as the penguin.

penguin's foot

The penguin picks up speed. It shoots into the air, or **porpoises**. It grabs a quick breath before splashing back into the water. The penguin porpoises towards the shore. This keeps it ahead of the shark. The penguin shoots onto the beach.

And the winner is...

...the penguin! It was lucky this time. But it had better stick with its group next time. Being an **agile** swimmer saved its life. The shark is big and not as flexible as the penguin.

What are the Odds?

A great white shark catches its **prey** about once every two tries! It has to surprise its prey instead of trying to out-swim it. A great white can eat 11 kilograms of meat in a single bite!

Glossary

agile quick and flexible

blend when things mix together so that you cannot tell them apart

camouflage animal's covering that helps it blend in with its surroundings

carnivore animal that eats meat

cell smallest part of a living thing

pectoral pair of fins behind a fish's head that helps them turn

porpoise leap out of the water and dive back in while speeding forward

predator animal that hunts other animals

prey animal that is hunted by other animals for food

vibration shaking movement

zigzag several sharp turns to change direction

Find out more

Books

Animal Top Tens: The Oceans' Most Amazing Animals, Anita Ganeri (Raintree, 2008)

Animals under Threat: Great White Shark, Richard Spilsbury (Heinemann Library, 2004)

Penguins, Emily Bone (Usborne Publishing, 2009)

Websites

http://kids.nationalgeographic.com/ Animals/CreatureFeature/Great-white-shark
Visit this website to learn more about great white sharks.

http://www.antarcticconnection.com/ antarctic/wildlife/penguins/index.shtml
Find out more about different types of penguin on this website.

http://www.oceansforyouth.org/kidscorner. html
Go to this website to find out more about animals that live in the oceans.

Index